LOBSTERS

ANIMALS WITHOUT BONES

Jason Cooper

Rourke Publications, Inc.
Vero Beach, Florida 32964

PHOTO CREDITS
© Lynn M. Stone: cover, pages 7, 10, 12; © James P. Rowan: title
page, pages 8, 13; © Breck Kent: pages 4, 21; © Mary Cote:
page 15; © Herb Segars: pages 17, 18

Library of Congress Cataloging-in-Publication Data
Cooper, Jason, 1942-
    Lobsters / by Jason Cooper.
        p.   cm. — (Animals without bones)
    Includes index.
    Summary: A simple introduction to the physical characteristics,
life cycle, and habitat of members of the lobster family.
    ISBN 0-86625-572-9
    1. Lobsters—Juvenile literature. [1. Lobsters.] I. Title.
II. Series: Cooper, Jason, 1942-   Animals without bones.
QL444.M33C67   1996
595.3'841—dc20   95-26010
                                                          CIP
                                                          AC

Printed in the USA

TABLE OF CONTENTS

LOBSTERS

With its heavy claws and armor-covered body, the American lobster is a true tough guy. On the ocean bottom where it lives, the lobster is a **predator** (PRED uh tor), a hunter.

A full-grown lobster has little to fear — except the traps set by people hunting lobsters.

Each year thousands and thousands of hungry lobsters crawl into the cagelike traps. When lobster hunters haul up the traps, the lobsters are sent to market. There they are sold as food.

This Maine lobster has walked into a metal lobster trap

WHAT LOBSTERS LOOK LIKE

Lobsters are a favorite seafood of North Americans. When cooked, American lobster shells turn bright red. Live lobsters, however, have shiny, blackish-green shells with orange trim. The lobster's shell is firm, but can bend, like thin plastic.

A lobster has two eyes and a pair of whiplike **antennas** (an TEN uhz). The antennas are sensitive to touch and movement in the water.

American lobsters can weigh from 1 to 20 pounds.

A lobster's eyes and antennas help it hunt on the ocean floor

KINDS OF LOBSTERS

American lobsters are the best-known members of the lobster family. Several other **marine** (muh REEN), or sea, cousins of the American lobster are called lobsters, too.

Spiny lobsters, for example, live along America's southeast coast. They have the long, jointed walking legs of American lobsters, but not the big claws. Spiny lobsters have stiff, sharp antennas for defense.

Crawfish, also called crawdads and crayfish, look like tiny American lobsters. They live only in fresh water.

Spiny lobsters don't have the heavy claws of American lobsters

THE LOBSTER FAMILY

Lobsters belong to a family of animals called **crustaceans** (krus TAY shunz). Most of the crustaceans are hard-shelled.

Turtles are hard-shelled, but turtles are not crustaceans. Crustaceans have no bones, and their bodies are arranged in sections, like the bodies of insects and spiders.

Over 35,000 kinds of crustaceans live in the world, most of them in oceans. Lobsters and crabs are heavyweights among crustaceans. Shrimp and crayfish and many smaller animals are also crustaceans.

Crabs, in the sea and on land, are crustacean cousins of lobsters

Wooden lobster traps dry on the dock at Southwest Harbor, Maine

Banded coral shrimp is one of the lobster's smaller, colorful cousins

WHERE LOBSTERS LIVE

American lobsters live in the cold North Atlantic Ocean from Labrador in Canada south to North Carolina. They are often caught in shallow water, from 6 to 120 feet deep. The biggest — and oldest — lobsters, though, live in deep water.

Lobsters of all kinds like to hide in rocky, undersea shelters.

Divers in the Florida Keys catch spiny lobsters on coral reefs close to shore.

A spiny lobster peers from its rocky den on a Caribbean Sea coral reef

BABY LOBSTERS

As its body grows, an American lobster sheds its old shell and grows a new, larger one. While a female lobster is without her hard shell, she mates with a male lobster. Several months later she lays between 5,000 and 100,000 eggs. She carries the sticky eggs on her body. They hatch about 11 months later.

Baby lobsters are called **larvas** (LAR vuhz). They go through many changes before they look like adult lobsters.

American lobsters grow slowly. A four-year-old weighs only about 2 pounds.

Eggs cling like green peas to the underside of a female American lobster

HOW LOBSTERS LIVE

Lobsters stay hidden in their dark, rocky dens most of the day. They are active at night, when they hunt. They travel from place to place by walking or swimming.

Like some of the other simple animals, lobsters can grow back lost claws or legs. If a lobster's leg has been hurt, the lobster can leave it behind. Later, the lobster grows a new leg!

This 10-pound lobster was pulled by a diver from the dark corners of a sunken ship

PREDATOR AND PREY

When it is a larva, a lobster is easy **prey** (PRAY), or food, for ocean predators. As an adult, the lobster is usually the predator.

The lobster is also a **scavenger** (SKAV en jer). Like a crow or vulture, a lobster will feed on the bodies of dead animals.

Lobsters catch fish, snails, and sea stars. They also eat clams, other lobsters, and marine worms. When it can't find prey, a lobster eats plants.

A lobster makes a meal of a small fish

LOBSTERS AND PEOPLE

The firm, tasty meat in a lobster's claw and "tail" is a prize for seafood lovers.

Lobster boats in Maine and New Brunswick, Canada, and other places, catch tons of lobsters. Lobster hunters bait their traps, or pots, with dead fish. A hungry lobster can easily enter the trap, but it can't figure out how to leave!

Lobsters are also raised on "farms" in salt water ponds.

Glossary

antennas (an TEN uhz) — whiplike feelers on the heads of different kinds of boneless animals

crustacean (krus TAY shun) — a group of small, shelled creatures with boneless bodies in sections; lobsters, crabs, shrimp, and their cousins

larva (LAR vuh) — an early stage of life in some animals; the young animal does not look like the adult it will become

marine (muh REEN) — of or relating to the sea and salt water

predator (PRED uh tor) — an animal that kills other animals for food

prey (PRAY) — an animal that is killed by another animal for food

scavenger (SKAV en jer) — an animal that eats dead animals and scraps

INDEX